God's Covenants

Cheryl Durand

Illustrated by Geneva Durand

"Great is the Lord, and greatly to be praised;
and his greatness is unsearchable.
One generation shall praise thy works to another,
and shall declare thy mighty acts."
– Psalm 145:3-4

Text copyright ©2018 by Cheryl Durand.

Ilustrations copyright ©2018 by Geneva Durand.

www.genevadblog.wordpress.com

All rights reserved.

Printed by CreateSpace.

LEGO®, the LEGO logo, the brick and knob configurations, and the minifigure are trademarks of The LEGO Group, which does not authorize, sponsor, or endorse this book.

Design by Geneva Durand.

Table of Contents

Chapter One

God's Covenant to Preserve His Creation   5

Chapter Two

God's Covenant to Prosper His Kingdom   13

Chapter Three

God's Covenant to Prepare the Way   21

Chapter Four

God's Covenant to Provide the King   29

Chapter Five

God's Covenant to Pardon and Save   37

Chapter One

God's Covenant To Preserve His Creation

Is a marriage a covenant?

What is a covenant?

A *covenant* is a promise, commitment, or agreement between two or more persons. People may lie and break their promises but **the Lord always keeps His covenants.**

(Deuteronomy 7:9)

In the beginning, God told Adam not to eat of the tree of the knowledge of good and evil, and that if he ate of it he would "die the death." That was a command with a promise of life if he obeyed.
(Genesis 2:16-17)

Could Adam disobey God's command?

Adam and Eve did eat of that tree. They brought sin and death to all. Even the ground was cursed and now thorns would grow and work would be hard. But **the Lord is kind** and revealed other promises.

(Genesis 3:15)

What new promises to man do you think God revealed?

What did man need now?

THE NOAHIC COVENANT

About 4,500 years ago, God made a *covenant* with Noah and his sons and all their future families. This means that you and I are part of this ancient *covenant*.

(Genesis 9:1-17)

Who is part of the Noahic Covenant?

Have you heard how God destroyed everything in the world by water? The Flood was God's judgment against sin. God saved Noah and his family in the ark. This was all part of the *Noahic Covenant*.

(Genesis 6-8)

Besides his family, who or what else was on the ark with Noah?

The Lord is kind and He promised that He would never again destroy the world with a flood. This meant that God would faithfully preserve His creation until the Lord Jesus Christ had come and until all His people have entered His Kingdom.

(Genesis 9:11)

What did God promise in the *Noahic Covenant*?

The rainbow is the token, or sign, of this promise. When you see one in the sky, remember this *Noahic Covenant* and that **the Lord always keeps His covenants.** *(Genesis 9:13)*

What should you remember when you see a rainbow?

Chapter Two

God's Covenant To Prosper His Kingdom

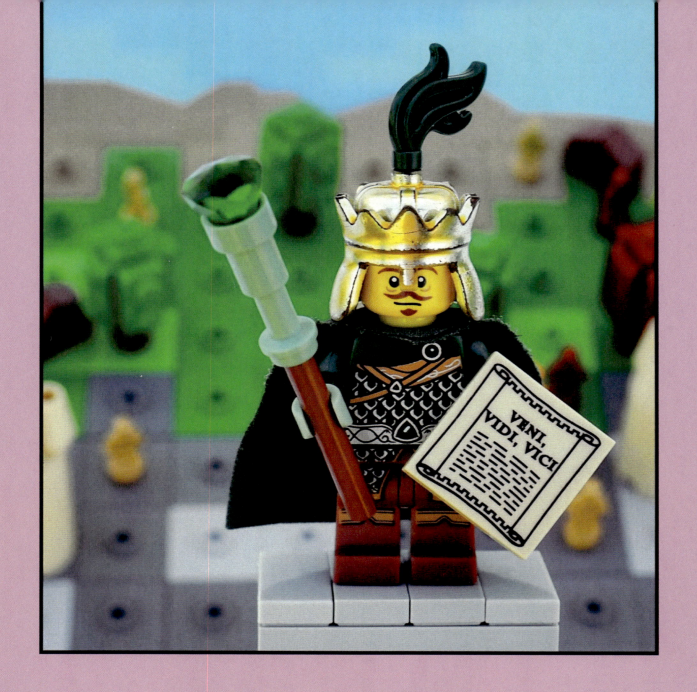

There are three parts to a Kingdom:

a <u>king</u>,

his <u>people</u>,

and their <u>land</u>.

What are the three parts of a Kingdom?

THE ABRAHAMIC COVENANT

Remember, a *covenant* is a promise, commitment, or agreement between two or more persons. **The Lord is kind**, so about 4,000 years ago He proclaimed a *covenant* with Abraham and his children.

> He would be their God (<u>King</u>),
>
> They would be His <u>people,</u>
>
> And He would provide a <u>land</u>.

What does the name Abraham mean?
(Genesis 17:5)

Which of the three parts of a Kingdom did this name represent?

The LORD always keeps His covenants.

The LORD promised Abraham that his children who followed him, the people of His KINGDOM, would be as many as the stars in the sky.
(Genesis 15:5)

How many stars are in the sky?

Does God know all their names?
(Psalm 147:4)

Does He know all His children?

This *Abrahamic Covenant* has always involved faith. Abraham believed God. All who share his faith are known as believers, both Israelites and Gentiles (those who are not Israelites).

(Romans 4:3)

What is involved in the *Abrahamic Covenant*?

Where does faith come from?

(Ephesians 2:8)

If the Lord Jesus Christ is your God, your Savior and King, then by <u>faith</u> you are a child of Abraham in God's Kingdom.

(Galatians 3:7)

Who is your King?

Does this help you know what Kingdom you belong to?

Until the time of the LORD JESUS CHRIST, circumcision, which is a cutting of skin, was the sign of this *covenant* and was a picture of the need to have sin taken away and be changed to love God, the King of believers.

(Genesis 17)

God told Abraham to leave his country to go to a different land.

Which of the three parts of a KINGDOM was this?
(Genesis 12:1, 13:14-15)

Those today that come under this *covenant* are baptized with water. This is a sign of their need to be cleansed from sin and born again to love God. When you witness a baptism, think upon God's promise to prosper His KINGDOM through the *Abrahamic Covenant* and the mercy of the LORD JESUS CHRIST.

(Galatians 3:27)

Are you a child of Abraham?

Have you been baptized?

Chapter Three

God's Covenant To Prepare the Way

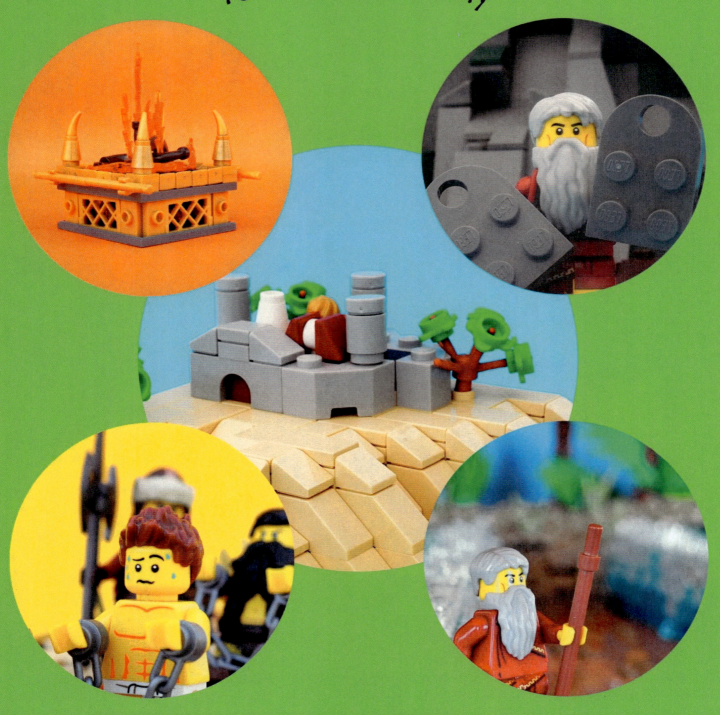

THE SINAITIC COVENANT

Through Moses, God gave the nation of Israel three types of written laws:

The Moral Law
(summarized in the Ten Commandments),

The Ceremonial Law
(such as the animal sacrifices),

The Judicial Law
(such as punishment for crime).

How did the LORD give the people His LAWS?

You remember how the LORD brought His people, the Israelites, out of Egypt after the ten plagues, through the Red Sea. Then, at Mount Sinai, God (the Redeemer-King) graciously entered into another *covenant* with His people, to give them the Promised Land on condition of *faithful* national obedience to these LAWS.

(Exodus 19 and 20)

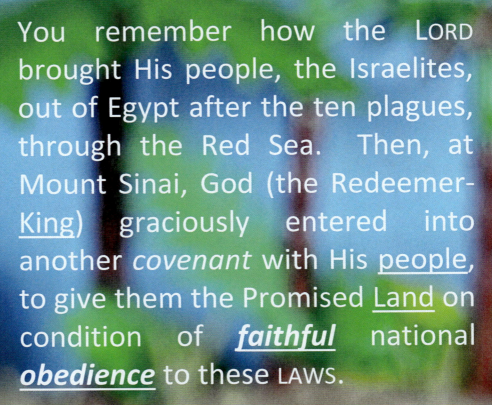

Were the people still blessed through the *Noahic* and *Abrahamic* Covenants?

(See Chapters One and Two)

If the Israelites listened and obeyed, many blessings were promised to them, including forgiveness when they repented. They would stay on their land and be an example to the world.

And the Lord always keeps His covenants.

(Deuteronomy 28:1-14)

What would happen if the people obeyed?

Wrath and curses, judgments for their sin, were threatened if they did not obey. This *covenant* would be broken if the people rejected God as their Redeemer-King and disobeyed His LAW. If they rejected God then He would reject them and remove them from the land.

(Deuteronomy 28:15-68)

What would happen if the people did not obey?

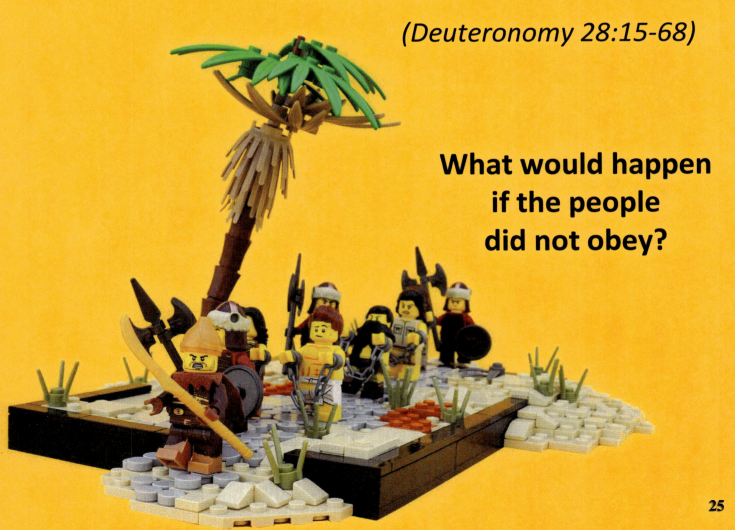

The Lord is kind and so this *Sinaitic Covenant* required <u>*faithful*</u>, but not perfect, <u>**obedience**</u>. Following the ceremonial law, the people were to bring sacrifices for personal and national sins and be reconciled to God. These sacrifices taught the people that all sin must be punished by death.

(Leviticus 4:2-4)

What should the people do when they realized they had broken God's law?

This is the story of the Israelites in the Old Testament: they fell into a cycle of sin, judgment, repentance, and renewal until the time of the LORD JESUS CHRIST.

(Psalm 44)

Does this cycle happen in your life?

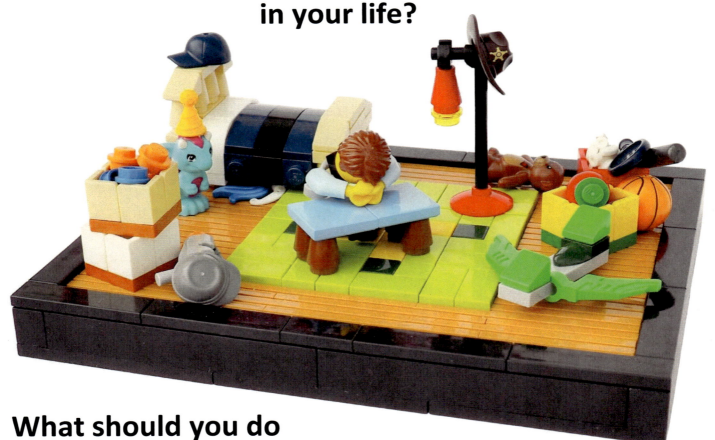

What should you do when you realize that you have sinned?

As you read the Old Testament, understand that the *Sinaitic Covenant*, the LAW, was showing people their sins and preparing the way for the coming of the LORD JESUS CHRIST and a better *covenant*.

(Galatians 3:24; Hebrews 8:6-7, 12:24)

How did the LORD JESUS CHRIST summarize the LAW?

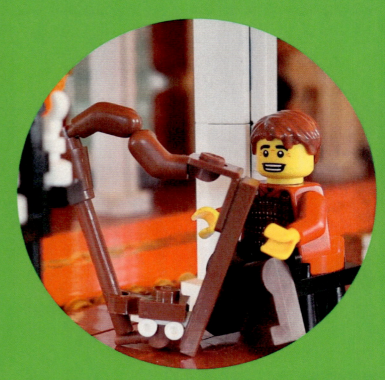

Chapter Four

God's Covenant To Provide the King

THE DAVIDIC COVENANT

The prophets, priests, and kings of the nation of Israel were ANOINTED, which means that oil, water, or blood were poured or put upon them.

(I Samuel 16:1-13)

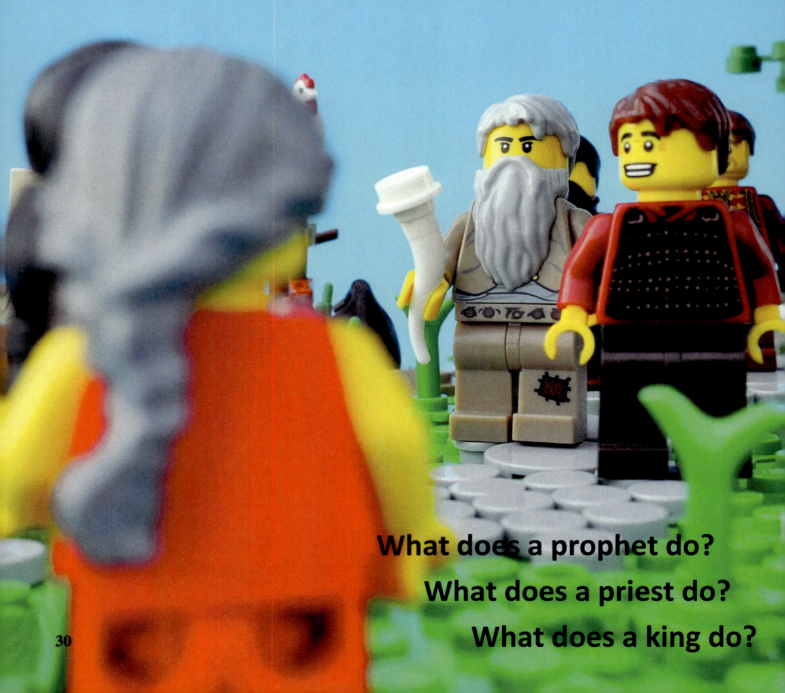

What does a prophet do?

What does a priest do?

What does a king do?

In the Old Testament, the kings were ANOINTED at God's command as well as received by the people. So the kingdom could pass from one family to another, as it passed from Saul to David.

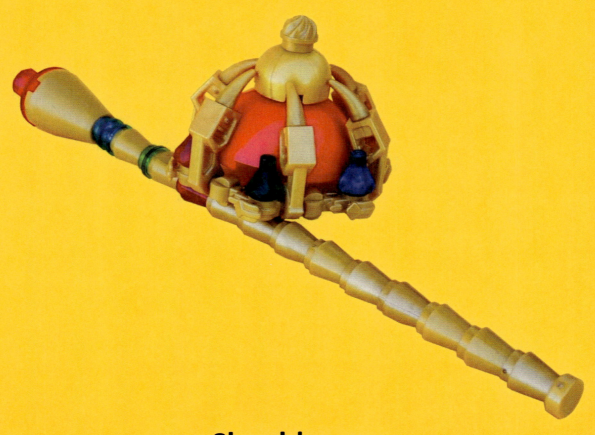

**Should a man
declare himself king?**

The Lord is kind and graciously made an everlasting *covenant* with King David to always establish some from his line of sons as kings and to build up his throne to all generations. Although this promise was made to David, its benefits obviously included those chosen sons of his who would be kings.

(II Samuel 7)

Would all David's sons be kings?

The LORD always keeps His covenants. This *Davidic Covenant* could not be broken. However, these kings could be judged for their sins and even cast down from being king.

(Jeremiah 33:25-26)

Although this covenant could not be broken, what could happen to one in the line of David's sons if he were a wicked king?

When JESUS was born, the Romans were ruling and some Jews had given up hope of a SON OF DAVID becoming king, while others still believed and were waiting for the promised MESSIAH, a Hebrew word which means the ANOINTED ONE. In Greek the word is CHRIST.

(Luke 1:67-73, 2:38)

What does the title MESSIAH or CHRIST mean?

The New Testament clearly proclaims that JESUS is this CHRIST, ANOINTED by the Holy Spirit at His baptism, the long-awaited SON OF DAVID, the KING OF THE JEWS.

(Mark 1:9-11; Matthew 1:1, 16:16)

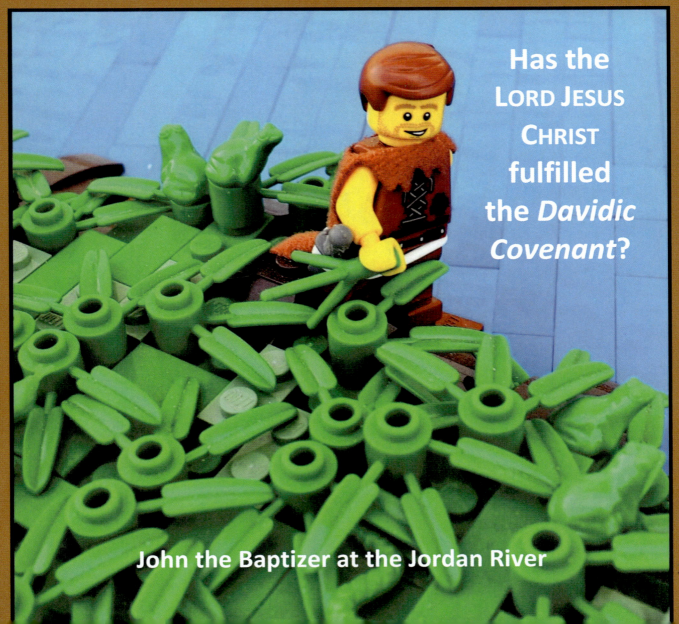

Has the LORD JESUS CHRIST fulfilled the *Davidic Covenant*?

John the Baptizer at the Jordan River

How has the Lord Jesus Christ fulfilled the *Davidic Covenant*?

When you read about this *Davidic Covenant* remember the Lord Jesus Christ and praise God for providing this Anointed King of Kings who will rule forever in righteousness.

(Psalm 72)

Chapter Five

God's Covenant To Pardon and Save

THE NEW COVENANT

The nation of Israel, as a nation, completely and finally broke the *Old Covenant* that God made with them at Mount Sinai by their public sin of rejecting the LORD JESUS CHRIST as their God, their Redeemer-King.

(Matthew 27:11-26; John 19:14-16)

What did the people say when the LORD JESUS CHRIST was brought before them at His trial?

God knew this would happen. He used it for good. The Lord has planned all things very carefully and all history shows that **the Lord is loving, wise, and kind**. So, knowing the sinful condition of all men, God had prepared a *New Covenant* with better promises.

(Jeremiah 31:31-34; Hebrews 8:6)

God promised to renew His people; to put His LAWS in their minds and write them on their hearts. He would be to them a God (King), and they would be to Him a people, a holy nation. How is this *covenant* better than the *Old Covenant?*

Can God change our desires?

Has He changed you?

This *covenant* is better because God Himself is with us in the Person of the LORD JESUS CHRIST. By His **_faithful obedience_** during His earthly life and **_perfect sacrifice_** on the cross He fulfilled the *Old Sinaitic Covenant*. JESUS lived a perfect, sinless life and transferred His righteousness to His people. JESUS – THE LAMB OF GOD – took the punishment His people deserved – He paid the penalty in full by His death on the cross.

Can you describe the double transfer that has taken place between the LORD JESUS CHRIST and His people to accomplish their salvation?

(II Corinthians 5:21)

The Lord Jesus Christ opened this *New Covenant* to include many more people from other nations, who by faith were added to the Jewish believers. Together all these children of Abraham would become one holy nation, the true Israel of God, the called-out Church of the Lord Jesus Christ.

(Romans 11; Ephesians 2)

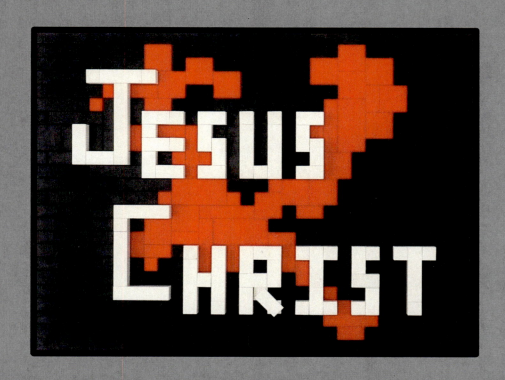

What does the name Jesus mean?
(Matthew 1:21)

Do you remember what the title Messiah or Christ means?

They are a people whose KING dwells within them by His Holy Spirit and gives them faith, repentance, love, and new obedience, with promises of a new heaven and a new earth in a completed KINGDOM of God.

(Isaiah 57:15; II Peter 3:13)

Where does our KING the LORD JESUS CHRIST live?

What do we remember at the Lord's Supper?

When your church celebrates the Lord's Supper, remember this is a sacrament of the *New Covenant* in which CHRIST's death is shown forth. Now, today, salvation is proclaimed because the KING has fully redeemed His people by His blood and righteousness, and CHRIST's resurrection celebrated every Lord's Day is our assurance that **the LORD always keeps His covenants**.

(I Corinthians 11:23-26)

What do we remember every Lord's Day?

Made in the USA
Middletown, DE
26 May 2024

54882309R00027